RIGGED

How Nurseries Can Significantly Reduce Workers' Comp Premiums, Legally!

By Mike McDonough

RIGGED

How Nurseries Can Significantly Reduce Workers' Comp Premiums, Legally!

Published by Maverick Mike Publishing

ISBN: 978-1-7351551-0-4

Cover design by Jim Saurbaugh | JS Graphic Design

This book is dedicated to many people who have been so gracious with their time mentoring me. First of all, my gratitude is to you, the employer, for reading this book. My mission is to get the message out to as many business owners as possible, so they too have the requisite knowledge to improve their company's bottom line.

My sincere thanks to my claims team for sharing their passion to help employers reduce their costs. A special thank you to my claims manager, Adriana, who believed enough in me to take me under her wing and mentor me. She has taught me so much, and with her help, she has made me a better broker. I want to thank Barry Bloom from the BDB Group for all of his professional insight on workers' comp claims management, providing tremendous insight on how I can truly lower my customers' claims costs.

I want to thank everyone who's invited me to various workers' comp trainings, seminars, and tradeshows. Through these networks, I have been able to connect with compatible professionals who share a common goal of helping injured workers and employers. I also want to personally thank all of the defense attorneys who took the time and had the patience to teach me about the legal process involved in workers' comp.

Also to all the claims examiners who work tirelessly making sure the employees receive their benefits and who have made a positive difference in the lives of thousands of injured workers.

And finally, to all the claims supervisors and managers for your willingness to help create and maintain a team concept with the common goal of making sure injured workers receive the care and benefits they deserve. And for taking the extra steps, setting up file and claim reviews in order for my employer clients to have transparency with their claims. This has provided a better understanding for all regarding how the system works.

Table of Contents

Foreword

For many in the business world, insurance is a necessary evil. Not many of us are experts in the mitigation of liability or in the process of managing workers' comp claims. We're experts in whatever our business sector happens to be, and since we're not experts, we must rely on experts in the field, namely agents and brokers.

If you're lucky, you end up with someone like Mike McDonough – the "workers' comp renegade." If you're not so lucky, you end up with someone who simply writes the policy, collects the commission, and is never to be seen again.

On January 8, 2020, I found out what an agent or broker **should be** in the person of Mike McDonough. One of our employees had a terrible and tragic accident in which he lost an arm.

After the ambulance left, I called Mike. He was at my facility within 45 minutes. The ensuing hours and days were a complete blur. I can tell you that if you ever have the misfortune of experiencing a serious work-related accident, your head will be spinning. Having someone to walk you through the steps of what you have to do in the aftermath is priceless – for both the employee and for the employer.

Mike has done a great job of articulating what you need to be doing ahead of time in terms of loss control and safety programs and in the aftermath of such events (even in the case of minor injuries) including appropriately managing the claim so that the employee gets the best care and treatment and the employer has control of future insurance premium increases.

This book is a "must have" road map to introduce you to the world of workers' comp insurance premiums and claims and to help you navigate the mitigation process and control premium costs. You will be very glad you read it!

Shawn Nutter
President
Apollo Wood Recovery, Inc.
apollowoodproducts.com

The System Is Rigged... Against You!

The topic of workers' compensation insurance can be both confusing and seemingly boring, yet a lack of understanding of its nuances can cause a nursery or any small business for that matter to close up shop. Too many businesses simply use their existing broker – who likely lacks the needed experience for workers' comp claims – and end up with a policy but little oversight or management on how to handle claims effectively in order to keep premiums from skyrocketing.

When a workers' comp claim is mishandled or improperly managed, it's like being in a taxi with the meter running. The doors and windows are locked, and you're stuck in the backseat, unable to get the driver's attention. The cab driver doesn't stop and the meter continues to run until the taxi runs out of gas. By that time, costs are excessive and extremely expensive. Depending on the case, those costs can bankrupt a company.

My goal with *RIGGED* is to explain the industry and what you need to know about workers' comp to ensure you have the right coverage at the right cost in a way that is clear, brief, and easy to understand.

Let me start by drawing an analogy with blood pressure. Physicians provide a baseline of 120/80 or lower as normal and healthy. A systolic (first number) value at 130 or 140 may raise an eyebrow, but when that number approaches 200 or higher, it's time for immediate action.

When the diastolic (second number) gets into the 90s, again, it's time for immediate action; otherwise, the patient is in danger of a stroke or heart attack. Treatment typically includes medication, dietary changes, exercise, smoking cessation and other lifestyle changes, and regular checkups. Once blood pressure is controlled and brought back into the normal range, you can live a fairly normal lifestyle. Ignore high blood pressure and life expectancy is shortened.

There is a very similar gauge for employers to take the pulse of their business health in regard to workers' comp – the experience modification rating or MOD. Like a healthy blood pressure reading, you want to have a healthy MOD. An admirable goal is .50, but more realistic goals are closer to .70 with a baseline at 1.00. MODs below the baseline mean lower cost, and numbers above that translate to higher premiums. Like elevated blood pressure, when a MOD score is 1.25 or over, the employer is getting well into the danger range, and it's time to take action. With MODs in that range, you are paying 60 percent more in premiums, which means your insurance broker is also receiving 60 percent more in commissions.

Also like blood pressure, when the MOD remains high, it could be catastrophic to a nursery or any small business when they're forced to close up shop due to the high cost of premiums. And to draw the same parallel, there are things employers with high MODs can do to improve business health like:

- Better hiring practices
- Healthy work culture and environment
- Strong safety and loss control programs

- Regular safety training with safety as a priority and never an afterthought
- Return-to-work programs
- Proactive claims management (working with an insurance professional who understands work comp claims inside and out)
- Transparency and communication with employees
- Claim reductions – occurrence and value

Patients diagnosed with high blood pressure require a lifestyle change. The same is true with nurseries and other employers with high MODs. They need to make a change to the way they handle all of the safety aspects of running their businesses, and just like the patient with hypertension, they can't go back to doing things the old way or their MOD score and their premiums go up to unsustainable levels.

Who's Who

All licensed doctors have completed medical school, but not all of them have the same skills. Those doctors who are primary care physicians are likely board certified in family medicine. They're generalists who are the right provider for basic health care. They can evaluate problems but do not have the skill and training for more in-depth treatments, like surgery for example. In those cases, they'll refer you to a specialist.

The same is true for attorneys. All have completed law school, and passing the bar allows them to practice law. However, that doesn't mean every attorney is the right choice for every case. If you have a legal issue that involves a tax or real estate situation, you'll want an attorney who specializes and has more in-depth knowledge in those areas.

The insurance industry works the same way, although every insurance broker who holds a property and casualty license is also licensed to sell workers' comp policies to any business. No special license required. But as with doctors and attorneys, you will always be better served with a specialist than a generalist. There are brokers who primarily write personal lines (life, home, auto, etc.) and may offer to write commercial policies for their personal lines clients; however, they don't necessarily have knowledge of commercial insurance, especially workers' comp. Similarly, brokers who write commercial policies often don't fully understand workers' comp insurance either. They lack the right specialty and most do not understand workers' comp or the true costs and risks associated with it. Like the family doctor or general practice attorney, these brokers are not your best choice when it comes to the specialty of workers' comp.

Maverick Moment:

Whether it's treatment by a doctor, advice from a lawyer, or workers' comp insurance, you will always be better served by a specialist.

If you have issues with your bones, you see an orthopedic doctor; real estate issues, a real estate attorney;

tax issues, a tax attorney. You get the picture. So when it comes to workers' comp insurance, you should use a true specialist who understands all aspects of workers' comp and how each factor affects the direct costs to you, the employer. When it comes to workers' comp, working with a generalist is financial suicide for your nursery.

Why Me?

I've earned the moniker, "Maverick Mike" in the world of workers' comp, and I'm passionate about it because I learned a long time ago how the industry works and how business owners are often overcharged for coverage. (All states are different, and I'm based in California where overcharging tends to be particularly egregious.) The system is actually built around everyone in the system (brokers, attorneys, health care providers, etc.) making money... except you – the employer!

Workers' comp was designed to help workers injured on the job cover expenses for medical treatment and lost wages. That's basic, and you already understand that. Unfortunately, states have made it incredibly complicated and have added layers upon layers of complexity. For example, in California, injured workers can hire attorneys and workers' comp is not tort law with punitive damages, etc. The hired attorney receives a fixed percentage of the benefits awarded to the injured employee, typically 15 percent of the settlement. ***In actuality, the attorney is taking part of the employee's benefit***... and most employees do not understand this. As an example, in a case that's settled for $40,000, the attorney's fee could be $6,000, meaning the employee only receives $34,000. Additionally, the applicant attorney also gets paid for depositions and all appeals board appearances, including hearings, conferences, and other related costs.

On-the-job injury leads to involvement by doctors, medical facilities, insurance agents, attorneys, claims examiners, defense attorneys, and the list goes on. There are a lot of moving parts and that includes brokers as well. In California, we have CIGA – the California Insurance Guarantee Association. It's very similar to a government bailout for insurance companies that fail to manage their losses appropriately. On every premium, employers pay a surcharge percentage of their total annual premium into this fund – which is billions of dollars, by the way. The fund is in place in case an insurance company has so many claims that their loss exposure exceeds their profits, leading to bankruptcy. When that happens, the injured workers still have to be paid, so the claims are paid out of the CIGA.

According to the code, the surcharge is paid by the member insurer (aka the insurance carriers) "through a surcharge on premiums charged by insurance policies." It further states that the surcharge amount shall be separately stated on the billing or declaration page *sent to the insured*. That's you, the employer. For the fiscal year 2011, CIGA paid in excess of $234 million in claims arising from insolvent member insurers, and for the five-year period from 2007 to 2011, the CIGA payout exceeded $1.4 billion, an average of approximately $280 million annually. I assure you, these numbers have only climbed since then.

If you're paying attention, and I hope as a small business owner you are, you'll see this fund *benefits the insurance companies* by allowing them to take advantage of the market by undercutting competitors and charging lower premiums. They take a lot of money up front, taking the cream off the top for profits, etc., leaving only the rest for claims… and when there's not enough to cover claims, they file for bankruptcy and leave it to the CIGA to cover payouts. But let's not forget about where the CIGA money came from in the first place – from all the employers who are paying workers' comp premiums. They're the ones who ultimately bear the financial burden for the claims.

It's actually a guaranteed system that allows insurance companies to be pretty bold, charging premiums, knowing full well that by low-balling the market that ultimately the employers are on the hook, not them. In California, there's no way for employers to stop this practice. With this in place, it literally allows insurance companies to open their doors, low ball estimates and generate a lot of revenue coming in, take in a lot of profit, and then when a lot of claims come in, they close the doors and go out of business. And it doesn't end there. The following day, they can open a new insurance business under a different name.

These sorts of practices are exactly why I'm passionate about what I do and why I want to help you fully understand the system. Unfortunately, workers' comp has its own ecosystem, and inside that ecosystem there is no relief for the employer… you. Someone has to stand up for the employer, and that's where I come in. That's why I'm Maverick Mike and have also been referred to as the "workers' comp renegade."

The Maverick Approach

My approach is to work with employers to find them a competitive insurance policy, and then I become a strategic partner in their company so that when an injured worker files a claim, I'm notified and I work together with the employer to take control of the claim from the moment it's reported. For example, if an injury happens to an employee who faces a language barrier. I have a fully bilingual staff who understands the language and culture who can clearly translate the terms and jargon of claims, so there is clear communication. The most important aspect for all parties is to remove the stress that occurs with any injury, but that's also compounded if there is a language issue.

Maverick Moment:

Work-related injuries are stressful. My approach is to work to alleviate that stress for the employee... an approach that serves the employer as well.

It's important for the employee to first understand that they are not in trouble for getting injured on the job. Secondly, they're not in trouble for reporting it. Third, they won't lose their job. Fourth, they won't lose any money from the situation. And finally, we're going to get them the best medical treatment available. When we can address all of these concerns for an injured worker, especially one who faces a language barrier, and remove fear and anxiety right up front in the process, it helps the claim to process more quickly, the communication is clearer, the employee receives treatment faster, so recovery time and the return to work are faster, and morale is much more positive. It's win, win, win.

By advocating for **both** the employer and employee, we're managing the injuries better, and the ultimate result is that we are also managing the employer's cost. The number of claims affects the MOD, and the size of any claim also affects the MOD. The MOD score, like blood pressure, ultimately affects the employer and their ability to stay in business.

Honestly, when a nursery owner or any employer has a claim, most of the time, they really don't know what to do. As a first step, they'll send the employee to the nearest clinic or emergency room. The result may be that there's nothing wrong with the employee, and the employer is now on the hook for $2,000 in medical bills to determine there's no injury or a very minor injury. This is reported to the insurance company; the insurance company pays the medical facility; and then the insurance company reports the information to the state's workers' comp insurance rating bureau (WCIRB). The WCIRB collects premium and loss data on every workers' comp policy written in California. I call this bureau the "premium police," and they're certainly not looking out for the employer. They "determine experience modifications (aka MODs)… and provide useful analytical tools and information to various workers' compensation insurance constituents." In reality, they're helping the insurance companies charge higher premiums.

The WCIRB is not helping employers. The *less* information the bureau gets, the better it is for the employer. When the MOD goes up, so go the premiums!

As Maverick Mike, I work to ensure my clients don't take this first, very big misstep. Instead, I've set up a nurse triage system for all of my clients to use. When there's an injury, my clients call my triage hotline and speak to a nurse who's trained in occupational medicine. The nurse conducts on over-the-phone interview with the employee assessing the injury. ***In the case of minor injuries and when warranted***, they'll recommend self-care or at-home treatment (which is likely the very same clinic recommendation). As a result, the claim never enters the system. Of course, if symptoms persist or get worse, now it's time for a doctor visit… but not just any clinic. We use clinics that are in the occupational medicine system to contain costs rather than sending them to the emergency room where treatment costs are probably ten times higher. (Let me stress again, that this is the approach for *minor* injuries, not anything serious or life-threatening.)

The Maverick Mike approach takes all sides into consideration – employer cost and employee health. We also use a return-to-work program for cases in which the employee is treated by a medical facility. For example, if there's a lower back strain, the doctor will prescribe when and for how long the employee can work. Our employer clients are all trained on how to be "modified work" employers. In the case of the lower back strain, for example, the employee can return to work but with a different regimen. Depending on the physician's restrictions, the employer can report to the insurance company that they are able to accommodate the restrictions. The result? The employee stays on full payroll – a benefit to both employee and employer. The employee doesn't lose wages; the employer doesn't lose productivity.

There's another win for the employer by keeping the claim to medical only. If the employer doesn't have a return-to-work program (and most don't because insurance brokers don't teach this), the employee stays at home, collecting two-thirds of their salary on what's call TTD – temporary total disability. This now increases the amount of the claim, and the claim's status changes from medical only to an indemnity claim. When an indemnity claim is reported to the WCIRB, they in turn report to the carrier, and in turn, the carrier surcharges the employer's premiums. That's a win for the insurance company, but it's a huge loss to the employer.

With the Maverick Mike approach, we use our own triage and immediate reporting. In fact, 60 percent of the claims reported to McDonough Insurance never reach the carrier… because the majority of claims can be treated with self-care. Additionally, of the 40 percent that require medical treatment, 95 percent of those claims are medical only.

We keep indemnity claims and litigation at a low rate. Of course, the result of this is that we're keeping employers' premiums at a very low rate and actively helping them control their costs.

Even More Complexity

As you're reading and learning how the system really is rigged against you, there is yet another layer of complexity. In the case of an injured worker being terminated for cause or disciplinary reasons, in California, that employee can come back months later reporting an injury in what's known as a post-termination claim. An attorney can use a date prior to the termination as the date of injury and claim continuous or cumulative trauma (CT). For example, if the injured and now terminated employee claims they injured their back, that is the specific injury, and when the employer reports, for example, that they've worked for them for ten years, the CT claim can go back that far.

Of course, this is a big issue for the employer and increases the cost of the claim. On the other hand, it benefits the applicant attorney because they'll get a percentage of a much larger disability payment.

When cases are litigated, the Maverick Mike approach is to get together with the claims examiner, claims supervisor, employer, defense attorney, and my claims manager to discuss a strategy on how to shut down a claim. For example, if the injured worker may require future medical care or surgery, we'll work to settle the claim prior to the deposition because our goal is to buy the claim at a discount. In the case of a 55-year-old employee with a back strain, the doctor may suggest surgery due to a "pinch on L-5" or similar. That turns into the cost of surgery and rehabilitation, and there is always the possibility of an unsuccessful surgery leading to additional procedures. It's not a stretch for this to turn into a $150,000-$200,000 claim.

By being proactive, we might offer $25,000-$30,000 to close out the claim now. If the employee and their attorney agree and we settle the case for $30,000, we've saved the employer $120,000. Keep in mind, we're talking about an employee who was terminated and whose injury may or may not have occurred as reported… or at all.

Maverick Moment:

Our approach is always a proactive one – from helping the employer institute safety procedures to return-to-work programs to shorten claims.

That's only one of many strategies that we can and do employ. Ultimately, my team and I are true advocates for the employer. I had a client recently tell me, "Mike, the reason I'm with you as my broker is because you look after my money like it was your own." I'm proud to say he's right.

When injuries are reported to the carrier, based on the diagnosis and treatment protocol, they set up a medical reserve based on their experience with similar cases and injuries for the subsequent few months. Added to that are lost wages. Let's say treatment is about $20,000 and lost wages is $10,000, so there is $30,000 in reserve. This money is in the insurance company's reserve. The insurance company is legally required to keep this money on their balance sheet. There's even a name for it. It's called a Balance Sheet Reserve based on the accounting of the reserve fund. Balance Sheet Reserves refer to the amount expressed as a liability on the insurance company's balance sheet. They pull it out of the premiums they're taking in, and the insurance company is actually showing *less* revenue and money to the IRS. Over-reserving can result in an opportunity cost to the insurer, and under-reserving can boost profitability with more funds freed up to invest. Of course, that equates to fewer taxes owed.

At the same time, they report the claims information (especially the indemnity information) to the WCIRB. This organization, in turn, develops a calculation – the MOD – that they report back to the insurance company. Let's put example numbers to this: A nursery pays $100,000 in premiums with no claims. But their MOD suddenly goes to 2.00 based on a few claims, and their premium rates double!

As an employer, I know you're scratching your head right now, realizing how much the deck is stacked against you. But wait. There's more… and it gets worse.

Brokers get paid on a commission basis. Let's use ten percent as the average commission rate. (Sometimes it's seven or eight percent, but sometimes it's as high as 15.) In the example above, with the employer/client paying $100,000, the broker is getting $10,000 for the year. For that commission, the broker *should* be providing services and consultation, helping with claims, perhaps setting up a loss control program, etc. Unfortunately, there are a lot of brokers who don't provide any services other than placing the policy. So they're making $10,000, and they're not providing services to their client for that money.

You're probably starting to see how the example I just shared gets worse. With the client's premium now going to $200,000 due to claims being reported, the broker just doubled their commission. In the first year, the broker did nothing to receive the first $10,000 and didn't do their job to help the employer avoid the claim in the first place, so in the third year the MOD doubled, the premiums doubled (now with $200,000 out of pocket), and the commission doubled (effectively a bonus of $10,000 for *not* doing their job)… all with zero benefit to the employer.

As the maverick in the industry, I specifically look for nurseries and other employers who've experienced increases to the MODs and work to lower them again – from 2.00 back to below 1.00 and even substantially lower than that, in the case of employers with no claims who've been in business for at least three years (according to California standards). In reality, I'm doing a great job for my clients, lowering their premiums to the greatest extent possible, and subsequently earning less than my competitors.

Obviously, I'm different than most brokers, and **some people even think I'm crazy for my approach**. However, with the number of employers I'm helping, I get quite a lot of referrals, and the clients I have stick with me for a very long time. They see the value I provide, so they don't shop around. New businesses begin with a MOD of 1.00. After being in business for a prescribed length of time and without claims, I can help nurseries and business owners drive their MODs down to .80 or even .50… which translates to lower premiums and more on their bottom line. In California, anything over 1.00 is a surcharge, and there are some employers in the state with MODs at 3.00 or 4.00! Every MOD increase means employers are paying more than they should be… or can be.

Again, we go into each nursery's business looking for where we can implement loss control and safety measures, culture changes, translation services, and other proactive systems. First and foremost, all of these factors are in place to avoid injury in the first place. Once we set the system up, it runs remotely, so when and if an injury occurs, all of the necessary steps (triage, notifications, etc.) happen automatically 24/7/365.

For me, at the end of the day, it's about doing the right thing inside this crazy, rigged system. We're all about the employer, and once we're for the employer, we're also for the employees – trying to avoid injury and getting the fastest, best care if an injury occurs with the least amount of downtime (and lost wages) possible. With this structure, employees are working with their employers rather than against them. We treat everyone in the company with respect.

As Maverick Mike, it's really me against the industry and the workers' comp system. Admittedly, there are those in the industry who don't care for my approach and practices because it digs into their profits. I don't care about their opinions. I care about the employers who receive all the benefits they should as a result of our hard work and efforts. I care about the millions of dollars I save for them.

I step up to the plate for each client with whom I work, and you can believe, I'm going to swing for the fences!

Chapter One

Strike 1: Using a Shoehorn Strategy

There are three areas in which I see employers making mistakes when it comes to choosing the right broker for their workers' comp insurance, and I want to cover them individually to help you avoid striking out. The first is the one I call the shoehorn strategy.

A shoehorn is a handy way to get your foot in a shoe. However, by definition, it also means "to force to be included or admitted; to force or compress into an insufficient space; squeeze."

The shoehorn strategy is used by some brokers who are simply looking to get the business and take the commission without adding any other value. It's as far as they go. They suggest they can offer a better price or do a better job than your current broker. Yes, price is important to any business and the cost of insurance is another expense line item. However, the lowest cost workers' comp policy is never in your best interest.

Workers' comp policies are based on time in business, number of employees, payroll size, claims, and classifications within your nursery or other small business. There are carriers that specialize in certain classifications, like those found in nurseries, construction, manufacturing, hospitals, etc. and perhaps can offer better pricing to companies within these niches, based on their claims histories and specializations. There are insurance carriers that may be very good with restaurants and focus on that industry and, at the same time, there are companies that will write a policy for a restaurant without real knowledge of the industry… it's not their forte. As an employer, it may seem like a handy shoehorn to bundle all of their insurance policies with one broker. On the other hand, the broker is shoehorning another policy into the portfolio.

Too many times, brokers call prospects offering lower rates without even having seen the company's portfolio. They don't know how long the prospect has been in business or the claims history or types of claims. Perhaps they're unaware that there's been a downsizing in the company or that there is a buyout or merger in the near future. There's a lot they don't know, yet they still call the business to offer workers' comp insurance… based on price alone.

There's plenty of commoditization in the insurance industry for all types of insurance – auto, home, etc. Consider all of the advertising you see that always offers the lowest price or claims to be able to save you money. They make these claims without ever knowing anything about you, like your driving habits, previous accidents, age of drivers in your household, violations, type of car, etc., yet they can quote you a price. This same approach exists in workers' comp insurance.

Few brokers and virtually no employers really understand workers' comp, and most employers commoditize the insurance-buying process, leaving themselves exposed to overcharges and errors. They assign insurance markets and shop for the best price, but ultimately, gaps and errors in their programs continue to be overlooked.

When a claim hits, premiums skyrocket because there is no oversight or proper management of the claim.

Workers' comp is not necessarily complicated when it comes to placing the policy. This is why many brokers try to shoehorn their policies into as many businesses as they can – shake your hand, place the policy, collect their commission, and walk away until it's time to renew in 12 months. However, once that policy is in place, it's critical to understand the business owner, their company culture and size, their needs, and what exposures they may have. Next, with all of this knowledge, it's time to set up programs and systems that are proactive and in alignment with the nursery's or other business's needs.

Maverick Moment:

As an employer and with the right broker, you can control the cost of workers' comp coverage!

As a nursery owner, you know that every business with employees must carry workers' comp insurance. True. You may also understand that the policy is based on your industry and the size of your business. Also true. If your payroll costs go up, your premium goes up. Conversely, if you downsize, you get a refund. Your premium is based on your payroll. Again true. As a business owner, you may simply look for the lowest price, knowing that ***if you have a***

claim, your premium is going to go up … and that's just the way it is. False.

Most employers do not understand that workers' comp is a controllable expense. They don't know that they have leverage and have a voice. They also don't realize that they can get involved in the claim to the level at which they can dictate the direction and cost of the claim. Yes, there's a real lack of knowledge about the industry and how workers' comp works, and if every employer understood this, there would be a lot more brokers making a lot less money and a lot more insurance carriers with a lot less profitability. Many attorneys and doctors would also be making far less. All of these people who stand to make less have no desire to involve the employer. For them, the system is perfect just the way it is. For brokers, when claim costs go up, premiums go up… and they get a bonus!

Strategic Partnerships

Nearly all brokers across the country simply want to shoehorn in another policy, selling on price. Yes, it may be short-lived when employers cancel policies due to poor service, but brokers know they can always shoehorn in another prospect who's only looking at policy price.

This is how, as Maverick Mike, I'm different. We're not about shoehorning any nursery or other business into a policy that isn't really right for them. That said, despite not selling on price, we're not really complicated either. Our approach is to be a strategic partner, just like a CPA or business attorney, and help our clients run better businesses – more efficient and more cost-effective.

Maverick Moment:

The shoehorn strategy never works on behalf of the employer. We believe in strategic partnerships instead.

We implement our systems and bring in our team at no additional cost to really understand what the employer's needs are. Then we bring to the table exactly what they want. We don't tell them what they need. We listen and then give them what they want. When we see them skewing off course, we'll provide advice to help them realign back toward the center. We demonstrate how they can save money. When clients are willing to be involved and take accountability by setting up proactive programs, they control their destiny in regard to their workers' comp coverage and premiums.

Premiums can be a roller coaster. A nursery might be paying $50,000 annually, and then have a few claims over a couple of years, so it goes to $150,000 the next year. Then they work to get it back to $70,000 only to have it swing back up to $130,000 the year after that. This roller coaster effect – premiums going up and down every year or every few years – makes it very difficult to run any business efficiently.

Case Studies

It's important to look at a longer range, like ten years, to get a handle on what the MOD should really be. I had a company contact me, and their MOD was 2.23. When I went into the system and looked at a ten-year average, it was 1.70. In reality, I knew it should and could be much closer to .70, so they'd been overpaying on their workers' comp premiums for a decade! I'm sure if I went back even further, the picture would have been a lot worse in terms of the money they paid for premiums that should have been on their bottom line or in the owner's retirement account instead. In my estimation, their premium overpayment was in the neighborhood of $1.2 million over those 10 years. Sadly, their broker was a friend of the family based on their culture, and they opted not to make a cultural shift and didn't hire me. Using a broker who's a friend or relative but who doesn't understand workers' comp is financial suicide for any business. With the MOD averaging 100 percent more than it should, the broker is being bonused for poor performance year after year. Where is the incentive of this so-called family friend to help this business owner? There is none. They'll continue to overpay, and that's their choice.

In another case, I was referred to another employer that had several open workers' comp claims, most of which were litigated. One included a serious injury suffered by an employee who fell two stories, landing on his back and head, suffering head and spine injuries as well as broken bones. Reserves were set at well over multiple-seven-figures, and close to a million was already paid out in medical only. This injury had occurred a few years prior, and miraculously, the employee has been released back to work. However, the claim isn't near settlement yet as the employee continues to receive regular physical therapy. The doctor hasn't deemed him permanent and stationary yet. (Permanent and stationary means that, in the doctor's opinion, the patient has reached a point at which their medical condition will not improve.). Once he is maximum medically improved, he will receive a disability payment of six figures plus future medical as he does have health issues resulting from the fall. There has been no oversight on this claim from the day of the injury by the employer's broker.

For the employer, the good news about the claim is that the employee isn't represented, and I'm still working closely with the carrier and claims examiner to reduce the reserves because most of the medical has already been paid. When I took over this account, I started digging deep into the claims with my own claims manager, and I looked for correspondence between the insurance company, employer, and broker. There was none, and it was fairly obvious there had been little to no communication through the entire process. I sent the examiner an email with many questions since this was such a large and serious case. The examiner didn't like my questions, and rather than replying to my email, she contacted the employer (now my customer) and asked, "Who is this guy?!?"

The employer's answer: "He's our new broker, and we want him asking these questions. We want to know and understand why these claims are so out of control and why our MOD went from .97 to 1.63."

I'd explained that the average MOD for this size employer could be as low as .70, perhaps lower. At 1.63, they were overpaying by 93 percent. With a new MOD of

2.29, their total surcharge was 159 percent. In 2019, they paid 159 percent more in premiums because of their losses that no one was monitoring or managing. Those premiums were in excess of $400,000.

Another case involved an employee who was continuously tardy and often arrived hung over. He was given fair warning and told if it continued, he would be terminated. When he showed up late and hung over again, he was released from the company. Then he filed a post-termination claim… that had zero oversight and incurred medical bills nearing $100,000 with no mention of a work injury prior to his termination and no medical records to substantiate or support it. The claim closed out at $177,000 and was litigated.

The broker wrote all the lines of coverage for this company including liability and excess liability, company vehicle coverage, property, and, yes, workers' comp. Most likely, this employer provided payroll and loss information and took the most competitive quote. When I asked, they admitted the broker had not been at all involved with the claims. He did his job placing the policy but that was the extent of it, and the policy may have been placed simply as an accommodation to meet mandatory requirements. The employer was completely in the dark and tried to handle the claim to the best of their ability without knowing who to talk to, what to do, how to review costs associated with the claim, etc. Having taken over their account, the good news is this is the only claim still open and should move toward closure and their MOD was issued for this year (2020) at 1.35, and their premium was reduced by $100,000.

Maverick Moment:

A broker may mean well when they write and place a policy, but they probably don't have the experience needed to effectively manage claims when they occur.

Unfortunately, I know there are countless stories like this and could talk about them all day long. Many employers trust their brokers to have their best interest in mind. I'd like to believe that's true; however, I know that most brokers do not have the experience and knowledge to understand employers' needs and to guide them through the process once a claim occurs. You know the saying: "You only know what you know, and you don't know what you don't know." It's true for employers when purchasing workers' comp policies, so they don't ask the right questions because they don't know what to ask.

The shoehorn strategy can be easy – for the broker. But it really should be about understanding the customer and what they want and then being there for them throughout the process, understanding their culture and implementing proactive systems (better hiring, triage nursing, return-to-work programs, attorney selection, etc.) to control costs when claims occur. Buying on price only works if you ***never have a claim***. Unfortunately, most employers don't know that I exist. And the truth is, it doesn't cost any more to hire me than it costs to hire any other broker.

In the same way that your CPA is there for you when you receive a notification from the IRS or your attorney reviews a contract before you sign it, we're there to make sure our clients are putting the pieces in place to mitigate and manage claims. We view ourselves as part of their company, even though we're not on the payroll. Our commission is probably the same as most other brokers, but our service goes well beyond what others offer. That's why they call me Maverick Mike, and I don't want you to swing at the shoehorn strategy.

Avoid Striking Out

- As an employer, it may seem like a handy shoehorn to bundle all of your insurance policies with one broker; however, unless the broker specializes in workers' comp, it's a big mistake.
- Most business owners don't really understand workers' comp, which makes it critical to use a broker who understands it through and through. Don't shop on price.
- Placing the policy is not complicated, but managing claims effectively when they occur is critical to keep premiums from skyrocketing.
- As an employer, you can actually control the cost of your premiums. You have both a voice and leverage.

- The Maverick Mike approach is to work with you as a strategic partner.
- Your broker may mean well and be a "nice guy or gal." That doesn't mean they have the knowledge and experience to help you when it really matters.

Chapter Two

Strike 2: No Dating Allowed

Workers' comp may seem simple, but it is not. It is the most misunderstood policy that is also the most costly if not managed properly. When there is a lack of understanding of how it really works, it can be one of the most expensive items on a business owner's balance sheet.

When you're "up at bat" in selecting your workers' comp coverage, I want to help you avoid swinging at the errant pitch I call "no dating allowed." In many ways, this builds off the previous one we covered. It's about relationships.

In social situations, when you meet someone, you want to get to know them before proceeding with any sort of relationship. You may find someone interesting at a party, but you may not immediately ask them on a date. You strike up a conversation; you may email or text afterward before proposing a date, and that first date may simply be to meet for coffee. You continue to date, maybe going to the museum, for a hike, and out for a nice meal. Maybe the relationship progresses to the point of taking a short trip together. You are spending time getting to know one another. What are their likes and interests? Where did they grow up? What's their personal history? How did they choose their area of study or career?

You are taking the time needed to get to know someone. The more you get to know about them, the clearer your decision becomes about spending even more time together… to the point of deciding to spend your life together and getting married. For some people, this may take a few years, and for some people, it may happen more quickly.

Now imagine meeting someone at that party who, by the end of the night, is trying to convince you that you should get married – tomorrow… without any dating, without getting to know each other! You really don't know anything about this person, so how could you make such a decision? Despite the idea of "love at first sight," it's a rash approach to such an important choice.

Some brokers work like this. They don't want to go through the dating process to build a relationship. They meet you and want to get you to the altar to consummate the deal. No questions asked. Yes, it happens socially as well. Perhaps two people meet at a bar, have a few drinks, and quickly escalate the relationship, but that doesn't mean it's a good idea. It's not a good idea when it comes to selecting a workers' comp broker either.

The Maverick Mike approach is to work with clients who want and need our services. Now by law, anyone with employees must carry workers' comp, so you might think that every employer is a "match." Not necessarily. Not every employer wants to work with us, and, at the same time, every prospect is not the right fit. If someone is shopping strictly on price, they are not a match for us. We've learned over the years that when someone buys on price, they leave on price as well. There is no loyalty and certainly no relationship.

This is even true for "blind dates" – referrals from other clients. When I get a referral from a client, I always ask for feedback regarding why that client thinks we'll be a good match. If you've ever been set up on a blind date, you've probably asked the person doing the matchmaking about the prospective date. What are they like? What are their interests? Why do you think we'll hit it off?

Well, I do exactly the same thing for referrals. I want to know about the conversations my client has had with the prospect. I want to be certain the prospect understands how I operate and the typical clients for whom we work. We're vetting each other, exactly the way you might before agreeing to go on the blind date.

Maverick Moment:

To work, relationships have to be the right match for both sides of the desk.

Here's what one of my referred clients wrote about us when referring us to another company: *"Our workman's comp program was in shambles and mismanaged by the prior insurance carrier for three years and we left them. We met Mike through a referral. He helped us to set up and execute an effective risk management and loss control program, introduced us to his claims consultant who micromanaged our insurer to clean up our existing claims. He moved us to a quality carrier which greatly reduced our rates, and most recently got us re-classified with the WCIRB into a lower premium insurance category. I'm on track next year to take my MOD down to about 1.00 or less under his guidance. Next year I expect my relative premium to fall in half from its peak. All the while, he has been a great communicator and educator. Frankly I can't say enough good things about him. With minimum wage increase coming up, it's more important now than ever to control labor costs. I wanted to refer you and encourage you to give him a call and see if he can help you."*

When I meet the referred prospect, I treat it like a first date. Ever been out with someone who only talks about themselves? It's not very helpful in terms of relationship building. As a broker, that is never my approach. It's not about what I need or want. I mention the referral and ask how I can help them. Then I shut up and let them do the talking. They'll quickly share with me the issues they have with their current broker, from a lack of returned phone calls to complete inaction when a claim occurs. No one answers any questions from why rates are going up to what may be happening with any or every claim. They have no idea what's going on.

Only when I fully understand what **they** want, will I begin to share how we help clients and how the Maverick Mike approach might benefit them. Again, it's about building the relationship first – asking questions and gathering information for both sides of the desk to ensure that there's the right fit before "walking down the aisle together."

Maverick Moment:

Beware the broker who does all the talking without understanding your needs and wants.

If there happens to be a mismatch and a referred prospect and I are not a good match (aka, we don't hit it off on the "blind date"), I do have other sources to which I'll refer them. They may not offer the same level of service, but it might match what the prospect needs for their budget. One way or another, I'll figure out a way to match the employer with the best service provider when I'm not the right fit.

One-Stop Shopping Is Never a Deal

There are now some payroll companies that have acquired insurance-licensed staff and are opening brokerages. They're soliciting their payroll clients, offering to integrate workers' comp coverage along with the service they're already offering and doing it on a pay-as-you go basis. It's seamless, so it *seems* like a good relationship to build.

Human resource companies are also doing something similar or payroll companies are adding HR divisions. They'll tell you, "In addition to the payroll and HR services we offer, we'll bundle it with workers' comp. You'll get that in addition to our legal services, onboarding employees, separation agreements, labor disputes, employee handbooks, etc." The nursery owner or employer may see this company as a great date… and partner – one company covering everything. One-stop shop. What could be better?

The problem is that a payroll company specializes in and knows payroll. If they've created an HR division, they probably don't know that very well. Ditto to their understanding about workers' comp. They're after the payroll business – their specialty and what they can deliver most profitably. Simply because they have other licenses, they can generate new revenue; however, they're probably not adding value for the client. In reality, bundling could be 20 to 25 percent more cost with less service. It's best to unbundle.

Despite offering "everything under one roof," they're not your best choice. When an injury occurs, there is no claims division to manage it. Instead, they turn the employer over to the insurance company with whom they've placed the workers' comp policy. Now that company is in charge – a company with which you have no relationship whatsoever and now the meter is running. And as we covered previously, when the premiums go up, their commission goes up as well. The employer gets frustrated and thinks "that's just the way the system is." Again, they have no idea that they can take control.

Additionally, because they're bundling these services, they may quote you a better rate without actually disclosing the actual costs. You might really be paying $10,000 annually for an HR template that anyone can provide. It's overpriced. As a nursery owner, it's actually better to unbundle and buy services from those who specialize in their respective areas.

Maverick Moment:

Companies that "add" workers' comp to their existing core competencies rarely provide the support and service you'll need when a claim hits.

To best serve my own clients, I have aligned with other service professionals (i.e., HR providers, payroll companies, etc.) who I know to be great at what they do and provide a service level similar to my own. As an employer, if you get a knowledgeable workers' comp broker (like me), and the great HR, payroll, and benefits providers I recommend, you are actually going to save money… and get the best of the best. Now that's a great match to which you can say, "I do!"

Case Studies

One of my workers' comp auditors referred a contractor who had an .84 MOD that recently jumped to 2.03. Guess who his broker is? A national payroll company. He's getting no service, and it's obvious from the emails he's receiving that the person handling the claim doesn't understand workers' comp. They're simply a mediary between this employer and the insurance carrier. When the employer poses a question, the payroll company employee has to send it on to the insurance carrier for an answer. The insurance carrier responds back to the payroll company who then responds to the employer. It's a really poor means of communication with the possibility of miscommunication of important information with every hand off.

I spoke to this business owner and asked the relevant questions. After a few minutes of conversation, he said, "Oh my gosh. You've helped me more in the last five minutes than the payroll company has helped in the last three years." He now sees the value. He has sustained three litigated claims that are open with incurred value of $200,000. Beware or at least think twice before hiring a payroll company as your workers' comp provider.

Another recent referral had a broker who wasn't managing claims, and it was readily apparent that he **wasn't** managing claims. Their MOD was high, and they had six open litigated claims. There was also a lot of frustration and a lot of questions: Why are employees suing? Why are these claims open? Why are the reserves so high? Within 15 minutes of a conversation and reviewing the claims with the employer, my claims manager and myself, this employer realized she'd outgrown her insurance broker, and I actually took on the account before the anniversary date, working for five months without commission. I became the broker of record and started to immediately make a difference – shutting down claims and turning things around. Out of six claims, there are only two left. Her comment was, "I would never have thought to send an email to my broker because he was never involved." She now sees the value.

Another employer had a 242 percent loss ratio with his previous insurance carrier when he was referred to me. He was with a broker and carrier that clearly did not understand workers' comp. We took him from in excess of 28 claims per year to eight the following year, and he went from $268,000 in incurred losses to less than $13,000 the next year. Based on his operation, we discovered that he'd been misclassified for multiple years. With our team's audit, we recovered $70,000 in returned premiums due to the errors and misclassification by the insurance company, and the carrier had to return the additional premium retroactively for the prior 12-month term. We also ordered an onsite inspection that led to reclassification, saving him another 30 percent off his rates. Because he now has a loss control program and safety programs and has reduced claims, we were able to get approval for additional credits. We saved him close to $200,000 in a single year and continue to help him keep his claims down, so his pricing drops every year. He certainly sees the value.

I have another client who has three claims, totaling $200,000 with a MOD published at 2.27. The client knew of the injuries; however, he was unaware of the amounts because no one had been communicating how bad the situation was. I pulled the losses (actual, redacted copies of them appear in the Resource section at the end) and shared them with him. He was in shock, not only by the amounts but because he'd been kept in the dark. He signed over his workers' comp account to us, and we took over as his broker.

These situations are so common, it's like Groundhog Day. Nursery owners and employers wake up and face the

same situations and frustrations about workers' comp over…
and over… and over… until they run into someone like me
who can advance the calendar to Feb. 3rd for them because I
know the business and understand exactly how the system
works. When brokers take the "no dating allowed" approach
and rush right to the altar, you can be sure the divorce rate in
that situation approaches 99 percent. It's a fast ball pitch and
one you definitely don't want to swing at.

Relationships matter, and it's all relationship based.
The stronger the foundation, the better it is for all parties –
the employer, the broker, and ultimately the employees. We
don't just manage claims. We educate our clients about the
process, so they're in the decision-making process along
with us. When employers become empowered and see they
are making decisions that are bettering their companies, it's
a real win. It's a match and marriage that can last. Kudos to
you for reading this book. I want you to understand that
people like me – workers' comp specialists – exist, so you
can stop kissing frogs to find the prince you need.

Avoid Striking Out

- It is always about relationships.
- Beware the person you meet who wants to drag you to the altar immediately and consummate the deal.
- We only work with clients who are the right "match" and consider referrals from existing clients very carefully. Not every broker can say that.

- Beware of those who offer one-stop shopping, like payroll companies that add workers' comp insurance. They are typically not a good deal for the employer.
- Unbundling, despite advertising to the contrary, can probably save you money in the long run.
- You will always find great value when you work with a broker who specializes in workers' comp and understands the system.

Strike 2: No Dating Allowed

Chapter Three

Strike 3: The Incentive

The third strike I want to share with you is a curve ball that I call "the incentive." It's when brokers swoop in with a low quote, followed by a "what-the-hell" approach. Like a pitcher with an arsenal of different throws, their goal is to strike you out. It's similar in the case of workers' comp – all of these strikes lead to the same thing: benefit to the brokers, carriers, and everyone else in the system except the employer – you, the nursery or other small business owner.

When workers' comp claims are mismanaged, the result can be so costly that smaller nurseries or businesses potentially go under. Their premiums can escalate to the point that they exceed the business owner's net profits. They not only strike out… they lose the game completely.

Simply put: workers' comp claims are a profit center for insurance companies. Let's say an employer pays the insurance carrier $100,000 based on his risk classification and losses. Two months later, a worker suffers a back strain while lifting or dislocates a finger. The employer reports the injury to the carrier, and the carrier assesses the injury based on similarly reported injuries. As we covered, now they set up a medical reserve. Based on the diagnosis and previous diagnoses with similar injuries, they presume the claim will clear within 60 to 90 days. The adjuster factors in office visits, physical therapy, the mileage an employee would be paid driving to appointments, and other expenses and sets the medical reserve at $10,000. If the physician assigns restrictions and places them on TTD (total temporary disability) so the employee is unable to work, the insurance company must reimburse the employee two-thirds of their gross income. Now it goes from a medical only claim to an indemnity claim. To keep the example simple, let's say the adjuster determines it will be another $10,000 for indemnity (i.e., lost wages). Now the reserve is $20,000.

This money sits in a reserve account. No one can use this money. It is there to pay the claim. Now the employee may heal faster than anticipated with fewer doctor's appointments or trips to physical therapy and return to work sooner, incurring fewer lost wages than originally anticipated. Let's say the total cost is $16,000. The employer gets the balance – $4,000 – returned.

Maverick Moment:

Workers' comp claims can be a huge profit center for insurance companies.

It's important to keep in mind that money going into reserves (and insurance companies might be funneling billions of dollars from premiums into reserve funds… and getting interest on this money) cannot be used for other typical operating expenses or other investments. More importantly, when the insurance company is filing tax returns, they are not reporting the money in reserves. They show less income, so they're paying less in corporate taxes.

Insurances companies have the reserves, pay less in taxes, and, depending on the number of claims, they share this information with the WCIRB to create a database of expected or average losses. As an employer, if your losses exceed that, you pay an additional surcharge. That's the basis of the MOD. When the MOD is 1.00, it's flat for you. No credit or debit. However, as we've covered, when a claim hits, your MOD goes up. In the case of our example, when the MOD goes to 1.25, that $100,000 in premiums is now $125,000.

So why do I contend that it's a profit center for insurance companies? Because they:

- Take in premiums.
- Set money aside for reserves on which they can earn interest.
- Show less income to the IRS, so they pay fewer taxes.
- Surcharge the employer for losses.

Where is their incentive to close the claim? There is none. It's a money maker for them. As I covered in the beginning, **no one** within the system actually has an incentive to close a claim when it occurs.

The Wrong Incentive

Even a third-party claims examiner or administrator (TPA) makes more when claims continue. For example, a self-insured employer hires a TPA and the TPA is handling the claim. The payment agreement for the TPA is usually driven by the number of files, services provided within those files, whether or not they have their own medical-provider network (MPN), bill and utilization review, etc. Their gross profit margin might be about 40 percent. The longer files are open and the more files they have, the more money they make. Additionally, when any of their services are used (e.g., MPN, utilization, etc.), they're getting paid.

To clarify this, let's say I'm a TPA handling an account for a national big-box store and there are 5,000 injuries per year. As a TPA, if I'm shutting down claims quickly and doing the right things for the employer and closely monitoring expenses (e.g., closing half of the 5,000 claims in one year), I just cut my income in half as I'm being paid per file. The longer the files stay open, the more money I make.

Maverick Moment:

The longer claims drag out, the more money there is to be made by those involved.

Employers (who haven't read this book) don't really understand how the system is working against them, so they don't question how long claims drag on. If a case goes to litigation, attorneys, of course, come into the mix. Like TPAs, they don't really have an incentive to close cases. The more claims they have and the longer those claims stay open, the more money there is to be made. *Let me repeat: no one*

in the system has an incentive to close claims... other than you, the employer, and me.

My goal in writing this book it to help you – the nursery owner or other small business owner – understand the system, so you can start asking the right questions to protect yourself. The Maverick Mike approach looks out for employers because I understand their challenges. If a defense attorney isn't handling the case expeditiously, we'll use a new one; request to sub them out if a claims examiner isn't moving things along, and we'll request the case be moved to another examiner; if there are issues that don't need to go to utilization review, they don't go. We also make sure employers "unbundle" to save money and evaluate their TPAs and defense firms to ensure they're using the best ones. TPAs may be using vendors who aren't necessarily the best financial decision on the employer's behalf and with whom they have no relationship.

This is also true of the employer's MPNs. Whether it's physicians, specialists, physical therapists, etc., they can all continue to bill "the system" or continue scheduling unnecessary follow-up office visits when the employee is fine and completely healed, causing cases to drag on. Again, there's more money there for them. Don't get me wrong. When an injury is such that expanded medical treatment and care are needed, so be it. However, I've seen a lot of minor injuries that don't warrant this extended level of care, yet it happens. A doctor may direct an injured employee to return for two, three, or four follow-ups that truly aren't need for the level of the injury. Unfortunately, no one questions doctors, and most employers simply follow doctors' orders. Once again, I am not second guessing the medical profession. What I want to underscore is the need to ask the right questions, and far too many employers don't: A) know they have the right to ask questions and B) know what questions to ask. Bottom line – the diagnosis has to fit the injury, so the Maverick Mike approach is to review this on every case. It's what I've hired my team (including bilingual translators) to do.

Injured workers are often fearful of losing their jobs because of an injury, so their first action may be to contact an attorney. Our team works to eliminate that fear by understanding that, in many instances, there could be a language or cultural barrier, so we explain the entire process in the language the employee feels most comfortable speaking, so the worker can get the right medical care and get back to work as soon as medically possible, assuring them they are not going to get in trouble or lose their job for reporting an injury. Our goal is to make sure they get the best medical care and don't lose any income. Once we do that, we eliminate the fear and stress that accompany a work-related injury. In turn, by looking out for the employees in this fashion, we reduce their likelihood of hiring an attorney by almost 90 percent.

The Right Incentive

Our incentive is to reduce the cost of claims. It is the right approach for both the employer and ultimately the employee as well. We direct employees away from visiting the emergency room or even an urgent care facility when they can get proper treatment elsewhere at far less expense.

We have all these systems in place and manage those systems so that when an injury occurs, it is handled properly from the very beginning. If they need emergency care, they get it; if not, we're not sending them for it. Additionally, we coordinate any needed temporary disability coverage to keep income loss to the very minimum for the employee. We make sure the employee gets what they need and that the treatment plan and medical care are always consistent with the diagnosis. Our goal is to help any injured worker heal 100 percent or to the degree possible depending on the injury and return to work in the most cost-effective way possible. When we do this, it works to the benefit of both the employee and the employer.

This is our incentive. We watch every dollar for our clients as if it were our own and manage every injury case for their employees, ensuring fair treatment and proper care.

When I have a client with a MOD of 2.00, the goal is to return them to a MOD of 1.00 or lower. When I take them from 2.00 to .80, I've reduced their cost by 120 percent. Yes, that also cuts my commission by 120 percent. Every time I reduce a client's premiums from $200,000 to $100,000, I cut out $10,000 in commission for myself and my team. Why do I do it? What's my incentive? Simple. ***It's the right thing to do.***

But by saving them money and being their advocate, they are quick to refer me and my team to others. We treat every employer – whether they have three or 3,000 employees – the same way. Every decision we help employers make is a strategic one that ultimately works for the financial best interest of the employer and health of the employee.

I don't know of any other business or industry where someone improves their own compensation due to the misfortune of someone else. When it comes to workers' comp, everyone in the system is actually incentivized and bonused when an employee is injured. With the Maverick Mike approach, we're not eliminating the other necessary players in the process (medical care providers, attorneys, etc.), but we are ensuring that they cannot and are not gouging employers. They'll get paid fairly and consistently, based on the injury and diagnosis. We align with those always keeping the employer in mind.

An injury is an injury, so we want to get the right treatment for the employee that ultimately benefits the employer as well. Regardless of the industry, whether it's in nursery or landscaping, an injury is an injury. If an employee breaks their arm in a restaurant, in a manufacturing plant, or on a landscaping job, the diagnosis is the same regardless the cause or industry.

Maverick Moment:

The goal is to get the right treatment based on the diagnosis, so it's fair to the employee and ultimately, the employer.

The difference to various industries regarding this injury is in the return-to-work program. If an employee breaks their dominant arm and their job description requires its use, work restrictions may have to be modified, so an employer may have to bring them back in a different position, capacity e.g., office versus warehouse, where they can perform functions that don't require use of the injured arm. Many times a job analysis is helpful in accommodating injured employees. Working with the employer to accomplish this, we help mitigate their exposure and cost and additionally benefit the employee by reducing or eliminating loss of income. We identify the return-to-work program when we onboard our customers, identifying the solutions before the injury occurs.

Does it work perfectly? No, of course not. There are times when even an employee's attorney tries to convince the employee to settle, but they have it in their head that it's a million-dollar injury. We cannot force them to settle nor can we force them back to work. Depending on the type of settlement an employee chooses, a claim can remain open for years. However, when this is the exception rather than the normal course of the claims process, the employer is still saving quite a lot of money. When these situations arise, we spend more time monitoring and constantly pushing for settlement. For the nursery owner, there's a big financial difference between having five or six claims open for four or five years versus having six claims with five of them closing down in months or within one year and only having one of them drag out. It becomes the difference in paying $500,000 a year in premiums and $100,000 a year in premiums.

Case Studies

I was recently referred to an employer with a MOD in excess of 3.00. This employer made decisions to contract out some labor to help save the company money in payroll. However, when six of these contractors were terminated, they all hired an attorney and filed CT claims (continuous trauma or cumulative trauma). We worked diligently with the employer's attorney to close out as many claims as possible in the shortest amount of time.

When these claims hit, they had no professional guidance, and these litigated claims could have been avoided with the right advisor. They had none, so the system beat them up financially. They weren't able to afford coverage, so they went without for several months. This lapse in workers' comp coverage has an analogous impact with insurance carriers that bankruptcy has on your credit rating. We helped the company turn around, and they're doing well today – claims are closed, MOD is trending in the right direction now at 1.70, and profit is growing. In the past year, no claims have been reported, and their premiums are below six figures and reducing.

Most employers do not see or understand the relationship between commission paid on workers' comp in relation to the value offered. Commissions are typically ten percent of the annual premium. Calculate that for yourself and determine what value you are receiving for that payment. All too often, it is none!

Partnership Incentive

When we work as a strategic partner and save nursery owners and growers hundreds of thousands in premiums, we become a huge value to our clients. At the end of the day, we align our clients with the best programs available and use our best procedures and systems based on their business and industry. We present everything available and help the client choose what will work best for them, from very conservative approaches to those with a bit of risk – not unlike investing in the stock market.

Some of our programs, like the one we offer for the San Diego County Flower and Plant Association, are exclusive by invitation only, and we're working with cooperative business owners who are dedicated to providing a safe and happy work environment. With everyone working together, implementing programs to reduce injuries, losses and claims, the excess pool of money created is returned to the business owner members to reduce premiums. Insurance companies are not offering these types of programs.

Why wouldn't an employer want to hire me as their broker or otherwise adopt the Maverick Mike approach? Namely, they don't understand the inner workings of the system and how it is so clearly rigged against them. There are other brokers who may take a similar approach, but probably not with the passion and conviction that I bring to the table.

What drives me is my ability to make a difference in people's lives by helping nursery owners and other small business owners run a more profitable operation; create a better, safer, and happier work environment; and reduce the stress and anxiety that rears up when an injury does occur. I have quite a lot of resources at my disposal, so I can become the central strategic partner for my clients. Everything we do is 150 percent with the employer in mind, with everything a financial gain or cost reduction to them. Yes, I get commissions, but I know those are commissions paid for a job very well done. I provide incredible value and service for the amount of my compensation. They get me and my team for the same price they are paying their current broker and get all my services included. In essence, they aren't paying any more money to have me as their broker. As a matter of fact, when I lower their premiums, they are getting me at a bargain!

My incentive, ultimately, is to provide solutions. Being the solution provider has earned me the nickname "Maverick Mike." It's one of which I'm very proud and work to maintain every day.

Avoid Striking Out

- Mismanagement of a workers' comp claim or multiple claims can cause a small business to fail.
- When an injury occurs, a reserve is set to cover the cost of medical treatment and possibly indemnity. This reserve is often a profit center for the insurance company.
- No one in the system – from claims examiners to medical professions to attorneys – really has an incentive to close claims. When claims drag on, they all stand to increase their own income.
- The Maverick Mike approach is to reduce claims and put systems in place to reduce the risk of injury in the first place.
- Like other brokers, I get paid on commission. My incentive to reduce my own income? It's the right thing to do.

Now that you've learned how the system is rigged against you, I encourage you to reach out to determine how we can work together to not only keep you from striking out but to actually swing for the fences and win the game!

Mike@McDonoughIns.com
www.mcdonoughins.com

Resources:

WCIRB Member List:

https://www.wcirb.com/sites/default/files/documents/2018_wcirb_membership_list.pdf

On the following pages are the actual loss records from a client who had been using a payroll company for his workers' comp insurance. Numbers don't lie.

Resources

Insurance Companies WC Loss Run

Report Date: 04/09/2020

Losses as of: 04/09/2020

Claim Claimant Adjustor Email Accident Type Description Injury	Date of Loss Received Closed	Lost Time? Pay Class Claimant Status Recovery Status	Employee Location		Medical	Indemnity	Expense	Total
	06/20/2016 06/21/2016 03/11/2019	Lost Time 5183CA CLOSED	001L	Paid: Outstanding: Incurred:	20,026.10 0.00 20,026.10	13,184.00 0.00 13,184.00	7,268.41 0.00 7,268.41	40,478.51 0.00 40,478.51
Internal Organs - Hernia STRAIN OR INJURY BY - Lifting								

Policy Summary

WC Loss Run Summary Sheet

Open/Closed	Med/Ind		Medical	Indemnity	Expense	Total
Total Open Claims: 0 Total Closed Claims: 1	Med Only: 0 Loss Time: 1	Total Paid: Total Outstanding: Total Incurred:	20,026.10 0.00 20,026.10	13,184.00 0.00 13,184.00	7,268.41 0.00 7,268.41	40,478.51 0.00 40,478.51

Report Date: 04/09/2020

Losses as of: 04/09/2020

Claim Claimant Adjustor Email Accident Type Description Injury	Date of Loss Received Closed	Lost Time? Pay Class Claimant Status Recovery Status	Employee Location		Medical	Indemnity	Expense	Total
	06/27/2018 06/27/2018	Lost Time 5538CA OPEN	001L	Paid: Outstanding: Incurred:	5,091.73 19,907.54 24,999.27	42,525.00 10,290.00 52,815.00	8,479.40 6,713.65 15,193.05	56,096.13 36,911.19 93,007.32
Low Back Area (Lumbar & Lumbo-Sacral) - Strain FALL OR SLIP INJURY - From Different Level								
	05/11/2018 08/16/2018	Lost Time 5538CA OPEN	001L	Paid: Outstanding: Incurred:	9,421.63 22,515.02 31,936.65	165.00 25,000.00 25,165.00	4,625.37 5,905.01 10,530.38	14,212.00 53,420.03 67,632.03
Multiple Body Parts - Multiple Physicial Injuries Only FALL OR SLIP INJURY - Miscellaneous								

Policy Summary

WC Loss Run Summary Sheet

Open/Closed	Med/Ind		Medical	Indemnity	Expense	Total
Total Open Claims: 2 Total Closed Claims: 0	Med Only: 0 Loss Time: 2	Total Paid: Total Outstanding: Total Incurred:	14,513.36 42,422.56 56,935.92	42,690.00 35,290.00 77,980.00	13,104.77 12,618.66 25,723.43	70,308.13 90,331.22 160,639.35

Total for All Policies

Open/Closed	Med/Ind		Medical	Indemnity	Expense	Total
Total Open Claims: 3	Med Only: 1	Total Paid:	35,050.42	55,874.00	20,440.72	111,365.14
Total Closed Claims: 1	Loss Time: 3	Total Outstanding:	42,911.60	35,290.00	12,951.12	91,152.72
		Total Incurred:	77,962.02	91,164.00	33,391.84	202,517.86

Resources

About the Author

Michael McDonough is owner of McDonough Insurance Services, a full-service insurance brokerage that specializes in workers' compensation insurance. Other lines of insurance include general liability, business property, commercial auto, and excess liability.

McDonough Insurance is known nationally for its outstanding workers' compensation coverage management. Mike has over 35 years of experience protecting clients from waste, fraud, and paying outrageous premiums in the workers' compensation arena. He serves the following industries: nurseries, flower growers, landscapers, and others.

McDonough Insurance provides the following services in the workers' compensation arena:

- Managing workers' compensation open claims. Working with injured workers to navigate the workers' compensation system and manage their claims in a manner that benefits both employer/employee and reduces overall cost. (Coordinating medical care, return-to-work programs, employee, advocacy, etc.)

- Evaluating employer equipment and premises to analyze safety concerns and implement safety practices as well as improving safety practices.

- Helping employers vet and hire appropriate employees who are less likely to file workers' compensation claims.

Made in the USA
Middletown, DE
16 July 2020